EVANGELISM JESUS-STYLE

REDEFINING THE WAY JESUS DOES EVANGELISM THROUGH YOU

STEVE PIXLER

EVANGELISM JESUS-STYLE

REDEFINING THE WAY JESUS DOES EVANGELISM THROUGH YOU

STEVE PIXLER

Published by
Continuum Ministry Resources
5200 David Strickland Road Fort Worth, TX 76119

Published in the United States by
Continuum Ministry Resources
5200 David Strickland Rd.
Fort Worth, TX 76119

Unless otherwise identified, all scripture quotations are taken from The Holy Bible, English Standard Version, copyright © 2001 by Crossway Bibles, a publishing ministry of Good News Publishers. Used by permission. All rights reserved.

Printed in the United States of America
Cover design by Chad Townsley

ISBN13: 978-0-9796261-8-0
ISBN10: 0-9796261-8-8

Library of Congress Control Number: 2013933524

TABLE OF CONTENTS

INTRODUCTION

Let's talk about the spirit of evangelism. It will only take a moment, and the things I have to say may change your life. Or, at least, change the way you do evangelism. This is a short book—no, let me be honest, "book" is rather pretentious: it is a booklet, no hiding that—and it will only take a few minutes to finish it and be on your way. But I assure you it shall be worth your modest investment of time.

Now, having seized your undivided attention, there are two things I want to say. First, the spirit of evangelism is the Spirit of Christ, the Holy Spirit, dwelling within you. You possess the spirit of evangelism whether or not you know it. If you are filled with the Holy Spirit, you have the spirit of evangelism. We shall talk about that further in a moment.

The second thing I want to say is that the spirit of evangelism that works in us as individuals becomes the spirit of evangelism that works corporately within a local church. There is a spirit of evangelism that sweeps through a congregation until it becomes the spirit and the culture of a local church.

But before we get into further detail about these two things I want to clear something up just a bit concerning evangelism itself. Evangelism is a fearful word these days. It provokes tremendous dread in the hearts of many believers.

Why is that? Because evangelism has been terribly mischaracterized and reduced from the full, rich concept of spreading the gospel in various, individual ways to a narrow, aggressive form of sharing the gospel that only a few can do successfully. Evangelism has been reduced to salesmanship and very few of us are good salesmen.

Evangelism these days can only be done by experts. Think about it now. Most of us have sat through sermons on soul winning where we left the building feeling utterly condemned. We were put on public trial and found guilty of failing to win people to Jesus. We were made to feel this guilt because we all know that we are called to participate in the work of evangelism. There is no doubt about that. The same passage that commands the church to baptize commands the church to make disciples. We can make evangelism no more optional than baptism. Both are essential.

And we have all heard over and over that the Holy Ghost was given to us so that we would receive power to become witnesses unto Him. So, we all know that we are supposed to be involved in the business of winning souls. Undeniable truth.

But this is where it all goes wrong. For the dominant model of evangelism that we all have been trained to follow is a salesmanship model, a marketing model, where the gospel is presented with charts and graphs, and we are pressured to close the deal and save a soul.

We are browbeat over and over that we must all be "soul winners," but the methods offered are those promoted by the outgoing extroverts among us, the people who never meet a stranger, those who do not feel the slightest bit embarrassed to stand up in the middle of Starbucks and preach the gospel over the heads of startled baristas and fleeing patrons.

However, most of us have never received the grace to witness quite like that. And since we cannot reach people *like that,* we think we are not good at evangelism. And we are ashamed.

Think about it now. If I told you now that you were required to do evangelism this Saturday, what would you expect to do? You would probably immediately envision knocking doors and inviting people to church. Maybe you would think of passing out tracts to strangers, preaching on the street corner or a half dozen other things that would make your palms sweat and give most of you the heebie-jeebies. Not all of you, but most of you.

Now, I am not minimizing these forms of evangelism. We need them all—for the most part. But what I am saying is that there are many ways to make disciples of all nations, and for the most part they involve very little public proclamation. Did you get that? I said that most evangelism involves very little public proclamation. No doubt, every seeker must hear the gospel publicly proclaimed at some point, but initially, at least, a lot of evangelism is done in private. Private preaching—now, that's something we all can do.

Here is the secret. Effective evangelism revolves around making friends. It is about those simple friendship-moments when you simply hang out with people, eat with them, laugh with them and become friends with them. Most evangelism happens around a meal, at a table in a workplace break room, squished in the middle seat on an airplane, or a thousand other places where we simply meet people and become friends.

Now, I am not saying we should not knock doors and preach on the streets. Not at all. I believe in all of that. I see evidence of this sort of public proclamation evangelism in the ministry of Jesus and the apostles, and I have done—and *I still do*—evangelism like that. So, I am not diminishing that. I am simply saying that there is much more to evangelism than just that.

My point is that there are loads of Christians who are not involved in evangelism because they have been led to believe that there is only one way to get it done right. As my Pappy would have said, "Hogwash." There are countless ways to do evangelism.

A while back, I preached a message to our church called "Evangelism Jesus-Style." Not only did this message have a really clever title, it was surprisingly effective. People, many of whom had been reared in the church, came up to me afterwards and expressed how much the message set them free of past concepts regarding evangelism. They were glad to hear that they do not have to be the Zig Ziglar of the gospel sales industry to fulfill their longing to lead people to Jesus.

In this message, I pointed out seven (later expanded to eight) examples of how Jesus reached people. Jesus did not reach people in just one way. He reached them through a variety of methods. This supports the notion that I am proposing here that Jesus wants to work *today* through different people in different ways to evangelize the world. If He did so in "the days of His flesh," He can do so now as He works through us by the Holy Spirit.

Let's look at several examples of "evangelism Jesus-style" from the Gospel of John. By the way, we could find numerous examples in the other Gospels, but we shall keep our focus here limited to John. We would not want our humble booklet to grow into a book and take on airs.

CHAPTER ONE

THE WEDDING AT CANA

John 2. The first example in John is the story of Jesus turning water to wine—or, fruit punch, if you insist—at the wedding of a couple of unlucky friends when they ran out of the wedding beverage. Now, there is no limit to the lessons to be drawn from this story, aside from making sure you have enough for your guests to drink on the big day, but we shall try to stay focused on the primary point here. What does this story teach us about the way Jesus did evangelism?

First of all, it teaches us that the opportunity to present the gospel arises at unexpected times in unexpected places. Jesus did not go to the wedding to work a miracle. In fact, He protested to His mother that it was not time to open His miracle career when she told Him of the dilemma with a meaning look. As mothers are wont to do, she ignored His protests entirely and instructed the servants to follow His instructions. As you know, Jesus obeyed His mother and saved the day. All very unexpected.

The second thing is that this was a simple social setting. Jesus was prepared to minister to people in everyday situations. This means that we must be prepared to do the same. We must not think that evangelism requires a bullhorn or a canvassing map. Jesus ministered to people wherever people were gathered together. We should do so, as well.

Third, Jesus ministered to His friends at the wedding "no strings attached." He made no demands of them. He simply met their need. Think about how we may do the same. We often find ourselves in social settings where people, for whatever reason, confide in us about their needs in their life and family. Hang around the punch bowl long enough chatting with friends, and they will open up a bit and tell you all about the current crises in their lives. This is evangelism just waiting to happen.

But we must be careful to follow Jesus here. Note that He did not think that it was necessary to require a *quid pro quo* in order to minister to them. It was "no strings attached" evangelism. Jesus did not offer to meet their need only if they would agree to a Bible study or come visit His church. He simply met their need without any demands. There is no record that He ever preached a sermon to the people swigging His wine. He gave freely in a grace-centered evangelism.

Of course, that does not mean that Jesus did not think that preaching the gospel was important. He came to seek and save that which was lost, and the lost are saved through preaching. But He also understood that evangelism is like farming, and it takes time to plant, water and grow a harvest. He did not mind doing long-term, slow-grow evangelism. He simply ministered to people wherever they needed help and trusted that those who were truly given to Him by the Father would be drawn to Him through His love.

So, what have we learned here? (1) That evangelism comes at unexpected times and places; (2) that evangelism often begins in simple social settings where we make friends and minister to their needs; and (3) that evangelism must be done by ministering to the needs of people "no strings attached."

Can you do evangelism like this? Can you hang out at the water cooler at work simply making friends and listening to the man whose marriage is falling apart? Can you drink a Diet Coke with a neighbor and be there when he or she needs someone to talk to? All you need to do is get involved in social settings, minister to people without any demands and watch as God makes you a magnet for hungry people that God is drawing to Christ. When the time comes, you can tell them about the gospel. But in the meantime, just turn their water to wine.

CHAPTER TWO

NICODEMUS

John 3. I see a great deal of our ministry situation in the story of Jesus and Nicodemus. Nicodemus was a religious man. He was curious about Jesus and His message concerning the kingdom of God. He was well versed biblically, and he had a genuine experience with God. But he needed more.

One of the most astounding things about this story is the discretion of Jesus. Jesus met Nicodemus under the cover of darkness so that Nic would not be embarrassed in front of his religious buddies. That is amazing. Jesus could have demanded that Nic take a stand and come to Jesus in broad daylight in full view of the Pharisees and hypocrites. But Jesus did not. He met Nicodemus on his own terms.

Now, let's sort out these two things. First, Nicodemus was a religious man. We often encounter people that are quite religious, people who have a deep, sincere relationship with God but are hungry to hear more about baptism in the name of Jesus and the infilling of the Holy Spirit. We have a choice: we can treat these folks like they have nothing with God at all, or we can follow the example of Jesus and allow our recognition of their present experience to form a bond that gives us influence in their lives.

Jesus called Nicodemus "a teacher of Israel." By doing this, Jesus both honored him for his position and grasped him by his rank in an appeal to his sense of responsibility to the truth. Jesus used Nic's love for God and Israel to draw him closer into the conversation.

We must do the same. We must recognize that virtually everyone who comes into the Pentecostal experience comes via other Christian denominations that do not embrace it. God leads people down many different paths to the full gospel. We must celebrate the faith that our "Nicodemus" holds and carefully lead them into "the way of the Lord more perfectly" (Acts 18:26 KJV).

Second, Jesus met with Nicodemus on his own terms. Jesus did not press the issue too quickly. He gave Nic time. He gave him privacy. Jesus did not impose an ultimatum prematurely. Jesus allowed Nic's faith to develop as he was able to grow in courage, and eventually, Nicodemus was numbered among the disciples of Jesus. (John 19:39)

So, how did Jesus do evangelism when reaching out to religious people? He recognized their experience as valid, as far as it went, and He met them on their own terms and allowed them time and space to grow in understanding. We should do the same.

CHAPTER THREE

THE WOMAN AT THE WELL

John 4. The third example of evangelism Jesus-style is the woman of Samaria that Jesus met by the well. The first thing that stands out in this story is that this was *not* random evangelism. John said that Jesus "must needs go through Samaria" (John 4:4), which is King James for it was necessary that Jesus pass through Samaria.

Of course, it could appear at first glance that this necessity was just a matter of geography—Jesus needed to go through Samaria just to get where He was going. The well was simply on His way. But the story indicates more. The story indicates that Jesus deliberately passed through this village because He had work to do here. Jesus made it clear to His disciples that He came to the well on purpose to do the will of God (v. 34). So, this evangelism was not random. It was specifically Spirit-led.

The second thing that stands out to me is that Jesus was willing to go into the rough part of town, as it were. This was an area of Palestine where Jews stayed on the freeway and passed quickly through. But Jesus exited the freeway and bought a Diet Coke—follow me, now—in the local convenience store where a little lady stood offering her services on the corner. Jesus went to the bad part of town.

Then, continuing to be led by the Spirit, Jesus struck up a conversation, to her total surprise (didn't this man know that his reputation could be ruined by talking to her?), and led her quickly into a conversation where the Spirit of prophecy unveiled the secrets of her life. This is Spirit-led evangelism through and through.

How often do we do evangelism that is Spirit-led? How often do we see the gifts of the Spirit, the word of knowledge, discerning of spirits, prophecy and faith, operating in evangelism? We are quick to display the operation of spiritual gifts in the safe haven of our local churches. But what would happen if we starting allowing the Holy Spirit to work freely in us while reaching for the lost?

And…well…anyway, as my wife's grandfather would say, Jesus spoke directly to her situation. He asked her about her personal life, and she realized immediately that He was a prophet. This made her uncomfortable, no doubt, and she changed the subject. She introduced theological controversy into the conversation, asking Jesus about matters of worship that had provoked conflict for generations. But Jesus never blinked. He did not back off the truth of the matter— "salvation is of the Jews" (v. 22)—but neither did He allow her questions to fluster Him. He spoke the truth, but He did so with love.

The Spirit led Jesus to the rough side of town. He allowed the Spirit to speak prophetically into her life. He did not avoid the tough theological questions. All of this is important to our understanding of evangelism Jesus-style. But the main point here, in my opinion, is that Jesus was willing to touch the untouchables, to reach the unreachables. Jesus was willing to tarnish His spotless record among the pristinely religious in order to save the lost.

Moreover, His willingness to get His hands dirty, as it were, allowed Him to reach an entire community by witnessing to one soul. Because Jesus was led by the Spirit and was willing to love the unlovely, He won the single person who had a story infamous enough to rattle an entire city (v. 39).

This woman was the key to a revival that shook the Samaritan countryside. In fact, the great revival that Philip preached in Acts 8 was a direct result of Jesus' witness by the well.

There really is no telling the sort of revival that we can experience if we are willing to reach out to the worst of our cities, believing that their salvation shall bring fame to our God and cause entire communities to believe.

Is our evangelism focused on reaching only the respectable people in our communities? Are we aiming for college-educated, upper middle class (and higher!) suburbanites that have a lot to offer the church? Or, are we willing to sit on the edge of a well in the roughest parts of town and reach for the outcasts that society has pushed away? Reaching the outcast is evangelism Jesus-style.

CHAPTER FOUR

FEEDING THE HUNGRY

John 5. And now, moving right along, we come to the fourth example of evangelism Jesus-style. This story is the one where Jesus feeds the multitude on the banks of Galilee, deliberately echoing Moses feeding Israel in the wilderness. Jesus made it clear for those who saw with the eyes of faith that He was the new Moses leading Israel through a new exodus into a new covenant.

Of course, many missed the point, but they certainly enjoyed the meal. Can you imagine being able to tell your children and grandchildren that you were *there* the day that Jesus fed over five thousand people with one boy's sack lunch. That would have been incredible!

But the main point for our study here is that Jesus was willing to do evangelism around a picnic table. He was willing to use food as means to draw people to hear the gospel. Of course, He condemned those who followed Him only for the fishes and the loaves, but that did not mean that He gave that feed-the-hungry-routine a fair try and then rejected it as a failure. Not at all.

Jesus later tells us that we shall be judged on whether or not we feed the hungry:

> Then the King will say to those on his right, Come, you who are blessed by my Father, inherit the kingdom prepared for you from the foundation of the world. For I was hungry and you gave me food, I was thirsty and you gave me drink, I was a stranger and you welcomed me, I was naked and you clothed me, I was sick and you visited me, I was in prison and you came to me. (Matthew 25:34-36)

The point, of course, is that feeding the hungry, clothing the naked, welcoming the stranger, visiting the sick and going to the prisons are all evangelism Jesus-style. This is not just a discredited "social gospel" that displaces the preaching of salvation by grace through faith. By no means!

We do not for a moment believe that we can save the world by feeding it. But we do believe that the hungry are more likely to listen to those who feed them. It is quite hard to hear the gospel over the rumbling of an empty stomach. I mean, think about it: we face that problem every Sunday morning just before lunch.

Seriously, now. We cannot lose the biblical mandate to care for the poor. We cannot lose the passion of Jesus to meet the needs of people. We must remember that He made meeting the needs of people with no strings attached the center of His ministry.

Jesus preached the gospel. Absolutely, He did. But Jesus preached more around the table eating with sinners that He did from behind a pulpit in a synagogue. And this is not to slight the need for pulpit preaching. Jesus did that, as well. It is just to say that we cannot allow a fear of liberal religious do-gooder-ism, politically driven community action and social gospel, pie-in-the-sky utopianism to stop us from feeding the hungry and helping the poor as a matter of evangelism. Jesus did so, and so should we.

Care for the poor is one of God's single greatest concerns. It is everywhere throughout scripture. Of course, God never intended for the care of the poor to become a government program where funds are taken forcefully from one and given to another. That is not charity. That is larceny. Government sanctioned highway robbery, if the Department of Transportation will forgive the allusion. But God did intend that society care for its poor. That much must be acknowledged.

James tells us that faith without works is dead being alone. But we really should read the entire context of that statement. The larger point is that we should help the poor. Look at it:

> What good is it, my brothers, if someone says he has faith but does not have works? Can that faith save him? If a brother or sister is poorly clothed and lacking in daily food, and one of you says to them, Go in peace, be warmed and filled, without giving them the things needed for the body, what good is that? So also faith by itself, if it does not have works, is dead. (James 2:14-17)

Faith without works is dead. What sort of works? Helping the poor. So, may we say it this way: evangelism without works is dead. Evangelism without helping the poor is dead. Evangelism without feeding the hungry is dead. Is your evangelism dead?

Maybe you cannot teach a Bible study. Fine. Maybe you hate knocking doors. No problem. Can you make a sandwich? Can you stir a pot of soup? Can you pass out shoes and socks? Can you help the poor? If so, then you can do evangelism.

Of course, feeding the hungry is not enough. They must hear the gospel. But I guarantee you this much, if you will get involved in helping the needy, you *will* have opportunities to tell somebody your story and share the gospel with them. I guarantee it!

CHAPTER FIVE

PUBLIC PROCLAMATION

John 7. Example five of evangelism Jesus-style is street preaching. Or, at least, it is public proclamation in various forms. Here is John's account:

> On the last day of the feast, the great day, Jesus stood up and cried out, If anyone thirsts, let him come to me and drink. Whoever believes in me, as the Scripture has said, Out of his heart will flow rivers of living water. Now this he said about the Spirit, whom those who believed in him were to receive, for as yet the Spirit had not been given, because Jesus was not yet glorified. (John 7:37-39)

Jesus "stood up" on the last day, the "great day," of the feast and "cried out." There are several things about this that fascinate me. First, the last day, the great day, of the feast was the last day of the year. It was New Year's Eve (on the Jewish calendar, of course). On this day, the priest would lead a great procession from the Temple down to the brook where he would scoop water into a golden vessel and take it back to the Temple to pour it on the altar of sacrifice.

As he did so, all of the people would quote with him from Isaiah, "With joy you shall draw waters out of the well of salvation." This is why Jesus rose to speak about living water that would flow out of the deepest soul of those who believe and receive the Spirit. Dramatic word, without a doubt!

The second thing that strikes me is that Jesus "stood up." Now, there would have been a tremendous throng of people in the procession to and from the river. So, when John says that Jesus "stood up," there is no doubt that Jesus climbed up on a wall or a ledge of some sort to get above the crowd. Maybe He used a soapbox. However He did it, Jesus demanded to be noticed.

The next thing that strikes me (is that my third strike?) is that Jesus raised His voice and shouted His message over the noise of the crowd. He "cried out." He cupped His hands and bellowed His message at the top of His lungs. If there had been a bullhorn handy, He would have used it. This is street preaching at its finest.

Now, think about all this. Jesus interrupted a religious ceremony, a ceremony that had become pointless and empty. The streets were crowded with people quoting scripture they did not understand. The passage they quoted was fulfilled before their eyes in the coming of Jesus and the promise of the Spirit that He would give. But they were too preoccupied with their religious rituals to see what was before them. They missed it altogether. Thus, Jesus took drastic measures to get their attention. He climbed up on a visible place and raised His voice to get their attention.

Now, how does this work for us? What is the best way for us to do public proclamation? No doubt, it could be done through street preaching. Street preaching certainly makes us visible and noisy. And there are times when this is exactly what we ought to do. For example, we have experienced great success with a mobile stage truck that allows us to preach the gospel in public places with great effectiveness.

But there may also be other ways to preach the gospel publicly. What about webcasts and other forms of electronic media? Technology has opened up a new universe of opportunities for public proclamation. What about print media? Is it possible to get the gospel out through mailers and door hangers? What about discussion groups and online forums?

The first century church often preached the gospel in the public square, the marketplace and the meetinghouses of that day. In our day, there are few public venues that we can use to share the gospel. In most cases, we cannot preach in the mall like they did in the market. But the few venues we do have should be used. We must get creative about it. We need to talk about it and share ideas. Whatever means we have for proclaiming the gospel publicly must be utilized to their fullest effect. Preaching in public is evangelism Jesus-style.

CHAPTER SIX

OPPOSING INJUSTICE

John 8. Now, here is an interesting example of the way Jesus did evangelism. Jesus saved the life of an adulterous woman who was caught in the act and brought to Jesus as a prop for the Pharisees to use in discrediting Jesus. It didn't work out so well for them, as you know. But the scenario provides a rich example of the way Jesus loved people and the lengths to which He would go to save them. Jesus hates the oppression of the weak, and His loathing for it comes through in this story.

There are two forms of oppression that Jesus exposed in this story: religious oppression and political oppression. The Pharisees that brought the woman to Jesus had behind them the force of the synagogue (the church, as it were) and the Sanhedrin (the Jewish civil government). But the proceedings were skewed. And the Pharisees knew better. They knew that their law required that both the man and the woman caught in the act of adultery be brought for judgment. But they had no concern for proper judicial protocol. And they had no concern for the woman's rights before God. They simply wanted to use her to discredit Jesus. She was a pawn on their religious and political chessboard.

Jesus, on the other hand, cared about the woman. He did not condone her sin. He charged her to repent, to "go and sin no more." But He would not tolerate institutional oppression, either. He first exposed the accusers as frauds and hypocrites. Then, He reached out to the woman in mercy.

This is fascinating. Jesus rescued a woman caught in the machinery of injustice, of a legal system skewed toward the powerful. He showed clearly that the powerful were as guilty as the weak, but the weak had no one to argue their case. Jesus played advocate, public defender, as it were, for the downcast woman, and before the day was done she was free from condemnation.

Now, what does this have to do with evangelism Jesus-style? Just this. We live in a world today that is still rife with instances of injustice. People in our society and around the world are caught up in the cogs and wheels of perverted justice and have no one to argue their case. God makes it clear throughout the prophets how He feels about the oppression of the weak and poor. He hates it! So, the church must take up the cause of the oppressed.

I do not mean that the church should join every politically and socially trendy movement that heralds itself as helping the oppressed. No way. The church needs discernment to know what is true oppression and what is political posturing.

But just because there are politically-driven movements that seek social upheaval in the name of justice, just because there are those who want to remake the world according their own vision of justice—a vision that usually places them firmly in control—just because there are corrupt people and institutions that operate under the banner of global justice does not mean for a moment that we should give up on the idea of delivering the oppressed. We simply need wisdom to know what is what in this fight.

Let me clear about this. I believe that the ministry of Jesus stands in line with the long tradition of the prophets, who cried out daily against the oppression of the poor. Go back and read Isaiah and Jeremiah. And that is just a good start. Read through all of the prophets, and you will find that God hates injustice. He hates it when the powerful use the power that He has given them—for all power is given by God (Romans 13)—to exploit the weak. *God hates it!* And if we are to be the people of God, then we must hate it, too.

James says, "Religion that is pure and undefiled before God, the Father, is this: to visit orphans and widows in their affliction, and to keep oneself unstained from the world" (James 1:27). We love to focus on separation from the world, but what about the first part? Pure religion includes helping the orphans and the widows, the weak and the oppressed. Where did James get this idea? From the prophets. And they got the idea from God. God cares about justice.

This bit on justice may seem odd in a work on evangelism, but we must see the connection. It is a part of the church's evangelistic task to make a difference in the world. Of course, this difference can only be made through the preaching of repentance and faith, baptism in the name of Jesus and the infilling of the Holy Spirit. Political and social solutions that are not rooted in the new birth are useless. In fact, they are worse than useless; they are damnable. But through the gospel the church has the power to make a difference.

31

The church must be caught up in the pursuit of justice in the world. We must work as advocates for the poor. We must get involved in the task of bringing clean water and healthy food to the hungry. We must build hospitals and clinics that bring desperately needed medical supplies to the sick and dying. We must get involved in preventing pollution of the water and soil where the poor live in every nation. We must pray and work against corporations that exploit resources on land stolen from native people.

We must help deliver slaves from those who buy and sell them. We must help stop human trafficking and the sexual enslavement of young girls around the world. We must help those wrongly imprisoned and unjustly sentenced to death for crimes they did not commit. We must work to end abortion and to stop the homosexual lobby from perverting the God-ordained institution of marriage as one man and woman for life.

This is a short list of big problems in the world that the church must see as a part of our evangelistic task. It will not do to quibble about a narrow theological definition of evangelism so that we can avoid the obvious: the gospel that we preach changes the world. You cannot preach the gospel without changing the world.

The gospel addresses man's relationship with God and with fellow man. All sins are social. All sins have to do with thoughts, words and deeds toward God and man. It is impossible to preach the gospel, to break the power of sin in the hearts of men and still leave systemic, institutional sin untouched. Since sin is social, the gospel is social. We cannot expect that the preaching of the good news of salvation would stop short of any area where sin has wrought its deadly work.

Jesus includes helping those around us in His definition of righteousness. The righteous man is one who feeds the hungry, visits the sick and those in prison (Matthew 25). As noted above, James sees helping the poor as the works that must follow faith. To reduce evangelism down to preaching that ignores the state of the world is silly. Can you imagine the prophets ignoring the sins of society? No way. Neither should we.

I really should bring this sermon to a close, but I need just a moment more to drive my point home. The musicians can come in a moment.

Paul's theology clearly teaches that the future envisioned by the prophets, when all things will be made new and the power of injustice finally and fully broken, has already broken into the world through the preaching of the gospel. In fact, the gospel that we preach is the good news that God has made all things new in Christ.

When we study the content of the gospel a little closer, we see that the gospel is the promise of a new creation, a new heaven and earth where righteousness dwells. This new world that is coming in the resurrection is a world where oppression is broken and sin is gone forever. It is a world where the poor are rich and the sick are well, where crime disappears and violence ends. It is a world where prisons are emptied, and war is waged no more. That is the world that is coming, and it is the world that has already begun to break into human history now.

Jesus was resurrected in the middle of history so that the future could affect the present *now*. The kingdom of God has already broken in upon the world, and it is having a present effect. Paul says in Ephesians 1:21 that Christ rules over "this age" and "the one to come." Jesus is presently the ruler of the kings of the earth (Revelation 1:5). The rule of King Jesus has already begun.

No doubt, the fullness of Christ's rule awaits the Second Coming, as Paul states in 1 Corinthians 15, but His rule has already begun. He has been given all power in heaven and earth (Matthew 28:18). The ascension of Jesus was the *inauguration* of Christ's rule. His Second Coming shall be the *consummation* of His rule when He shall have subdued all of His enemies and shall rule with His people forever in a new heaven and new earth.

This means that we should expect to be salt and light *now*, as the gospel forms God's elect people into a sanctified community within the world that models and mediates the age to come into the present age.

We must get involved. We must stand up with Jesus on behalf of the oppressed. Are they sinners? Yes. Is this the reason they are in the mess that they are in? Yes. And that is why they need to hear the gospel. We must lift the woman up from the ground and offer her hope: "Neither do I condemn you; go and sin no more."

This is a big subject, and it needs further discussion. But at least, we must not say that the good works listed above have nothing to do with evangelism. The gospel is the good news, and good news without good works is not good news at all.

CHAPTER SEVEN

MIRACLE-EVANGELISM

John 9. Now, let's get back into territory that we are more comfortable exploring. All that good works stuff makes us nervous. But miracles? Now, *that* we can appreciate.

John 9 is the story of the blind man that Jesus healed. Jesus was in the middle of a deep controversy with the Pharisees over His identity and mission. Just before Jesus healed the blind man, they threatened to stone Jesus for making Himself equal with God:

> Your father Abraham rejoiced that he would see my day. He saw it and was glad. So the Jews said to him, You are not yet fifty years old, and have you seen Abraham? Jesus said to them, Truly, truly, I say to you, before Abraham was, I am. (John 8:56-58)

That statement, "Before Abraham was, I am," was a loaded statement, and the Pharisees knew it. They caught Jesus' allusion to the God of Israel identifying Himself as "I AM," and they hated Jesus for daring to suggest that He was the embodiment of God.

However, Jesus was unmoved by their threats and walked undaunted through the midst of them, leaving the temple. As

He passed through the crowd, He saw the blind man. John says it like this:

> As he passed by, he saw a man blind from birth. And his disciples asked him, Rabbi, who sinned, this man or his parents, that he was born blind? Jesus answered, It was not that this man sinned, or his parents, but that the works of God might be displayed in him. We must work the works of him who sent me while it is day; night is coming, when no one can work. As long as I am in the world, I am the light of the world.
>
> Having said these things, he spat on the ground and made mud with the saliva. Then he anointed the man's eyes with the mud and said to him, Go, wash in the pool of Siloam (which means Sent). So he went and washed and came back seeing. (John 9:1-7)

As with all of the previous examples of Jesus' evangelistic ministry, there are numerous parallels that can be drawn out of this story. The first one is that Jesus worked this miracle as He passed through the crowd. He did not erect a tent and hang banners over the gate of the temple announcing that He would perform miracles at half past twelve on Friday afternoon. He did not make a production out of His miracle ministry. He simply passed through the crowd and responded to a need.

I think this is one of the most important aspects of miracle-driven evangelism. Too often, the quest for miracles among us is a desire to see sensational things and—more importantly—*to be seen doing* sensational things. Too often we seek for miracles because we lust for glory. But Jesus simply ministered as He walked through the crowd. How about it?

Are we willing to simply walk through the crowd and respond to an unexpected need with miracle faith?

There are countless opportunities for spontaneous miracles in our daily life and witness. If we would simply walk through the crowd and be sensitive to the needs around us, you never know when we might be given the opportunity to pray for the man with cancer, the woman in a diabetic coma, the child with inoperable tumors. If we would simply walk among those in need, at work, in the neighborhood, on the street, at the park, then we would see miracles.

The simple point is this. Miracles should be directly connected to the needs of people rather than our need to be sensational. Or even our need to be "apostolic." We should pray for miracles because people need help. Compassion must be the driving the force of miraculous power.

But there is more. Jesus worked this miracle as a sign to Israel. The healing of the blind man was a sermon. Jesus illustrated clearly that the Pharisees were blind and needed a miracle to see. However, they refused to look to Jesus in faith, and their blindness remained. When Jesus healed the blind man, He was making a statement about His power to heal those who believe.

Jesus' point about the Pharisees' blindness was powerfully demonstrated when they refused to glorify God for the miracle, even to the point of casting the formerly blind man out of the synagogue when he refused to denounce Jesus as a sinner. Who was truly blind here, the one who could not see with natural eyes, or the ones who *would* not see with spiritual eyes? I think Jesus made His point loud and clear.

But the larger point for our discussion regarding miracle-driven evangelism is that Jesus worked miracles as signs. He healed people because He loved people, no doubt. But He also healed people as an announcement of the coming kingdom of God.

This is why miracles are called "signs and wonders." Miracles are signs. Signs of what? Signs of the coming new creation when sickness and disease will be forever banished. Miracles are like signposts pointing to the city ahead. When Jesus healed the blind man, He was pointing to a time when both physical and spiritual blindness would be gone forever.

Miracles send a message. They announce to the world that the kingdom is coming. Thus, miracles must always remain grounded in the message of the kingdom. Miracles that are disconnected from the message of Jesus are self-gratifying, self-aggrandizing miracles that quickly degenerate into sorcery and witchcraft. Ask Simon the sorcerer about that (Acts 8).

This is why miracles are always connected to evangelism in the Scriptures. Miracles are prophecy. Miracles are preaching. Miracles are evangelism. Miracles tell a story, the story of Jesus and the promise that He shall make all things new.

Miracles are directly connected to the message and the mission. The mission of the church is to preach the gospel of the kingdom, the Good News that all things are new in Christ. The power to work miracles is given by God to the church in order to vindicate and validate this claim.

Our story is rooted in the resurrection of Jesus, and when we work miracles, we are demonstrating the resurrection in miniature. When we heal the blind and raise the dead, we are declaring to the principalities and powers that their time is up and their authority has been given to Christ. We are proclaiming to the world that Jesus is its rightful sovereign and that He is coming again to judge all nations. Miracles are meant to say a lot about Jesus and His work in the world. Miracles are not meant to say much about *us*.

Let me pound this point like a drum. (Ra-pum-pum-pum-pum.) Miracles facilitate the *message* and the *mission*. Jesus sent His disciples out into the world to preach gospel to all the *cosmos*. He promised them that miracle power would attend this mission. He kept His word, and the early church healed the sick, raised the dead and cast out devils as a means of attracting the world's attention to the message and mission of the Christian church.

Look at Mark's account:

> And he said to them, Go into all the world and proclaim the gospel to the whole creation. Whoever believes and is baptized will be saved, but whoever does not believe will be condemned. And these signs will accompany those who believe: in my name they will cast out demons; they will speak in new tongues; they will pick up serpents with their hands; and if they drink any deadly poison, it will not hurt them; they will lay their hands on the sick, and they will recover.
>
> So then the Lord Jesus, after he had spoken to them, was taken up into heaven and sat down at the right hand of God. And they went out and preached everywhere, while the Lord worked with them and confirmed the message by accompanying signs. (Mark 16:15-20)

"These signs will accompany those who believe." And "the Lord worked with them and confirmed the message by accompanying signs." This shows clearly that miracles are directly connected to the message and the mission.

If we are not seeing the miracles that we long to see, maybe it is because we have untethered miracles from their proper mooring of message and mission. Maybe we are too busy begging God to work miracles in our Sunday service for our own enjoyment rather than seeking miracles for our Monday morning outreach to the world. Maybe we would see more miracles if we reconnect our pursuit of them to evangelism.

I think this is one reason why there are so many dramatic miracles in mission fields around the world. No doubt, the miracles in faraway places have something to do with the simple faith of people in underdeveloped lands. But I think it also has to do with the fact that missionaries tend to seek miracles so that the message and mission will be vindicated and validated before unbelievers rather than just hoping to see God do something spectacular next Sunday.

Our common attitude toward miracles is sort of like the difference between using explosives for a Fourth of July fireworks display and using them on the battlefield to defeat an entrenched enemy. Are we seeking miracles for the "ooh and aah" or for the "Shock and Awe"?

One final point on this and we must move on before our humble booklet swells into a multi-volume desk set. The church in Acts understood very well that miracles were directly connected to their message and mission. When they were persecuted for the name of Jesus, they gathered in an upper room in Jerusalem and prayed until they were all filled again with the Holy Spirit and the house shook again with heavenly power.

Look at the record of their prayer:

> And now, Lord, look upon their threats and grant to your servants to continue to speak your word with all boldness, while you stretch out your hand to heal, and signs and wonders are performed through the name of

your holy servant Jesus. And when they had prayed, the place in which they were gathered together was shaken, and they were all filled with the Holy Spirit and continued to speak the word of God with boldness. (Acts 4:29-31)

They understood that healing, signs and wonders are performed through the name of Jesus so that the church may be emboldened to preach the gospel. Miracles accompany the message and the mission.

So what must we do? I think we should simply get focused again on evangelism, on walking through a crowd of people looking for those who are in need. If we will simply minister to the needy and preach the gospel to the lost, there will be ample opportunities for us to speak faith and work miracles. We must reconnect miracles and evangelism.

We should pray as the Acts church prayed. We should fervently seek God to confirm His word with signs following. We must not hesitate to ask God for miracles. But we must be careful that we seek miracles for the right reasons—for the message and the mission.

41

CHAPTER EIGHT

RAISING THE DEAD

John 11. One last example of evangelism Jesus-style, and we shall wrap this part up.

The story of Lazarus could be stretched out in a thousand different directions as an example of the way Jesus did evangelism. But, for me, the resuscitation of Lazarus immediately brings to mind the restoration of backsliders. They were alive spiritually, but they have fallen away into spiritual death, as it were, and they need to be revived.

Now, I have to be careful with the story of Lazarus because I am working on another book-length treatment of this story, and I cannot afford to bring too much of that material into this diminutive work if I am to keep it humble. And, of course, how will I sell you the forthcoming book if I give it all to you here? This is a stewardship issue, people.

Anyway, the story of Lazarus makes me think of how God restores backsliders. This is an important aspect of evangelism. That may sound odd at first, but think about it. People who backslide do so because they have lost their grip on the gospel. Either they have lost sight of the grace of God that saved them and no longer believe that they are forgiven, or they have lost sight of the urgency of the gospel and the certainty of divine judgment. Either way, the backslider needs to hear and believe the gospel again.

The church sometimes loses sight of the need to reach wayward children. It is easy to forget the prodigal in the hog pen. Out of sight, out of mind. No doubt, the story of the prodigal son has in mind the larger story of the Pharisees' rejection of sinners and Israel's rejection of its mission to the nations, but Luke 15 still applies to backsliders. Backsliders are the ultimate prodigals, and the church that neglects its obligation to reach backsliders is the ultimate elder brother.

In the story of Lazarus, Jesus delayed His response to the family's appeal for help. It may seem at times that this is exactly what happens with those who falter spiritually. It may seem like God does not come through in time to heal the ailing soul, and they die as a result. But never fear. Jesus has not forgotten our backslidden children. He will come when we call. It is a matter of timing.

When Martha heard that Jesus was coming and went out to greet Him, she lamented His late arrival. Jesus did not hesitate for a moment. He immediately launched into a rehearsal of the gospel, of the promise that Martha believed concerning the resurrection of the dead.

This is a powerful moment. If we trust God to save our prodigal children, we must look back again to the gospel. Only the gospel can save, and we must speak faith again to our children and about our children. The only hope they have is the gospel, and that is all the hope they need. Believe, Martha!

Just after Jesus' sermon to Martha concluded, Mary came out weeping to where Jesus waited on the outskirts of town. When Jesus saw her, He did not wind up a second sermon.

No, He began to weep. Softly, at first, then His grief erupted in loud cries of sorrow. But we must be clear: Jesus was not weeping for Himself or for Lazarus. He knew very well that Lazarus would live again. But Jesus wept because He loved Martha and Mary.

Jesus took up the cries of His friends and their cries of despair were transformed into cries of intercessory triumph. Jesus wept for them, and He weeps for us today. When we do not know how to pray as we ought, the Holy Spirit makes intercession for us according to the will of God (Romans 8:26,27). The only hope we have for our backslidden children is that Jesus prays in our prayers by the Spirit and makes intercession for them according to the will of God.

We must believe the gospel concerning backsliders. We must trust that the grace of God will bring them home. And we must never stop praying fervently for them. Martha, believe! Mary, intercede! God will raise your Lazarus again.

Now, here is the amazing part. Jesus allowed Lazarus to die so that God could be glorified in his resurrection. As surreal as it sounds, God permits our loved ones to wander so that He may be glorified in them. Does that sound crazy to you? But before you reject it, think about Simon Peter and his denial of Jesus. That is a great example of backsliding. Can't get much more backslidden than denying Christ. Yet, Jesus told Simon Peter that He had given Satan express permission to sift Simon as wheat. And Jesus assured Simon that He was praying for him that his faith would not fail. Which is exactly what we should be praying for our Christ-denying children.

The main point is that God used Simon Peter's defection from the faith to save him. And, if we can believe the gospel and trust in God, Jesus is able to use the backsliding of our children to save them. It is when we lose hope and stop praying in faith that their backsliding becomes final and fatal.

Just keep believing, Martha, and keep praying, Mary. Soon Jesus will stand by the opened tomb of your loved one and cry, "Lazarus, come forth!"

CHAPTER NINE

YOU *ARE* A WITNESS

No doubt there are other reasonable variations on how these events may be interpreted with regard to evangelistic models. But the point that I want to make with all of this is not that everyone must interpret these models as I do, but that we should see in this variety an obvious indication that evangelism cannot be reduced down to one particular method of reaching the lost.

In fact, the point I am getting at is that the spirit of evangelism is working in each of us individually *as* individuals. The spirit of God in each of us is a unique witness of the resurrection of Jesus in us. Evangelism should be done in you like you would do it. This is why God gave each of us His Spirit to dwell within us as individuals. God is glorified when we bear witness to the resurrection of Jesus in our own inimitable style.

If you can possibly bear to be put off a little longer, we shall look more closely at the idea of individual evangelism in a moment. But for now, get this point, and let it sink down into your ears: there are a thousand different ways to proclaim the gospel. Evangelism is simply the *euangellion*, the proclamation of the gospel, however it is done. Just because you are not proclaiming the gospel in the same way as Fred or Bill does not mean that you are not proclaiming the gospel.

What I would like to do here is liberate you to become the witness God called you to be without feeling like you have to do it within a certain evangelistic model. In what way are you good at serving people? In what way are you good at reaching out to people? In what way are you good at making friends? Then, that is the way that God wants you do evangelism.

Let's pursue this point a little further. My basic point is that all who are filled with the Spirit have the Spirit of evangelism in them. You may not have developed your outreach skills. You may not even understand the full implications of what you have in you, but you have evangelism *in* you right now just waiting to blossom.

Have you ever felt the desire to be a witness for Christ? Well, then let me set you at ease: you *are* a witness. Whether or not you even meant to be, you *are* a witness. If you are filled with the Spirit of Christ, then you cannot help but be a witness.

Not convinced? Think about it. You have the supreme Witness dwelling within you. I don't have to ask you today if you *are* a witness; I only have to ask if you have the Holy Spirit. *That's all I need to know!* For if you have the Holy Spirit, then you are a witness even if you are a relatively ineffective one.

Follow me, now. If a man standing on the sidewalk sees an automobile accident, he is a witness of the accident. It does not matter whether or not he is a good witness, but he *is* a witness. He may stutter and stammer on the witness stand. He may be embarrassed to say what he saw. The crowd in the courtroom may intimidate him. He may not be articulate and persuasive when he speaks, but he is a witness whether or not he likes it. He is a witness *because of what he saw.* Period.

This man doesn't need to become a witness. He needs to become an *effective* witness. He needs to learn how to share his witness. His problem is one of technique, of style, of method. If an easy-going attorney can put him at ease, he will spill the beans. All he needs is a setting where he can loosen up, where he is free to be himself.

Friends and neighbors! Did anybody get that? The same is true of evangelism. You are a witness simply because you have seen the goodness of the Lord. All you need is a little help understanding how to share your witness in your own way. Your problem is that you have been trained to believe that there is only one way to effectively witness. And in a different sense that is true. There is only one effective way to witness—the only effective way is *your* way!

This is why new believers are so effective in evangelism. They have not yet learned that you have to have a Masters degree in soul winning in order to do effective evangelism. They just simple bubble over with evangelism, an evangelism that flows out of their experience with God. They witness simply because they *are* a witness.

You cannot have the Holy Spirit dwelling within you without being a witness on some level, for the fact that you are filled with the Spirit testifies that God raised Jesus from the dead. The living Christ is living in you. You *are* a witness! You are living proof of the fact that Jesus rose from the dead.

We witness to the faithfulness of God. We are eyewitnesses of His glory. We may not have seen Jesus rise from the dead bodily, but we have seen His resurrection come to life within us when we were dead in our sins and He gave us life. We *are* witnesses.

And whether or not we testify effectively of our witness, we at least do testify on some level just by being born again and living a Christian life. The Spirit of God within you is Himself the Witness. The Testifier is in you. The divine evangelist is in you. Jesus is in your heart. And as the man said, "Let Him out!"

Jesus had a thing or two to say about all this. Look at what He said:

> But when the Helper comes, whom I will send to you from the Father, the Spirit of truth, who proceeds from the Father, he will bear witness about me. And you also will bear witness, because you have been with me from the beginning. (John 15:26, 27)

The Spirit will bear witness of Christ, and you will bear witness of Christ as a direct result of His witness. We may not be one of the original disciples that saw Jesus after He rose from the dead, but we do have the Witness of the Spirit within us. We witness because we *are* witnesses.

Let me say it again: You have the spirit of evangelism within you because you have the Holy Spirit within you, which *is* the Spirit of evangelism. Jesus said, "But you will receive power when the Holy Spirit has come upon you, and you will be my witnesses in Jerusalem and in all Judea and Samaria, and to the end of the earth" (Acts 1:8). Has the Holy Spirit come upon you? Then you have received power to be a witness. Have you received the Holy Spirit? Then, you have the Witness within you!

You have the spirit of evangelism in you. You simply need to know how to let Him grow in you so that you may witness of the resurrection of Jesus in a way that employs your unique gifts effectively until you help make disciples through your particular Christian witness. You are the only witness that only you can be.

That is profound.

Chapter Ten

You Are Gifted For Evangelism

So, then, you ask, why am I ineffective in winning people to God? Great question. My answer is this: you are trying to win people in ways that is not consistent with the gifts of the Spirit that God has placed within you. You are trying to win people by imitating successful "soul sinners" who are gifted in ways that you are not.

Simply ask yourself this question: in what way am I gifted to serve people? Then ask yourself if there is a way that you can serve unsaved people in this way. How can you put your gifts for service to work in an evangelistic way?

Are you good at preparing meals? How can you get involved in meal preparation for the unsaved? Are you good at listening to people as they pour out their troubles? How can you bring that gift into the service of ministering to unsaved people?

Now, we do not have space here to fill in all the blanks for everyone. Remember, we are trying to contain this booklet before it becomes an epic tome. You will have to work out your own salvation a bit here. Put yourself in the question: "In what way am I gifted to serve people?" When you answer this question you will have discovered your unique gift for evangelism, your way of reaching people that no one else can do.

People, I am saying without blinking that God has gifted everyone in the church to be an effective witness for Christ in such a way that they play a direct role in helping someone come to Christ.

Maybe you are not a home Bible study teacher. That's okay. Can you make the cookies and hang around afterwards to simply be a listening ear to those attend the Bible study? Can you take flowers to the hospital? Can you read scripture to the elderly in a nursing home? Can you be a friend to someone at work that needs to hear about Jesus and His mercy? Can you provide prayer support for the outreach teams that go out into the neighborhoods and knock doors? Cold-call evangelism may give you the heebie-jeebies, but some people love it, and they need your prayer cover. Everyone must get involved in some way in the work of making disciples.

The simple fact remains that most of us are not engaged in evangelism because we have seen evangelism as the soul winning success of evangelism experts, and we think we are not gifted to win people to Christ.

Yet, we all desire on some level to win souls. It is in all of us to make disciples because the divine Discipler dwells within us, and He longs to employ our unique gifts for His purpose. He came to seek and to save that which was lost, and He lives within us to complete that mission.

You will never be satisfied as a Christian until you are actively involved and fruitful in making disciples. But you will never be fruitful in making disciples until you realize that God filled you with His Spirit so that He might use you *as you* and not as others in the saving of souls. You have particular gifts that God has planted within you, within your personality, that He wants to use to save the lost. You simply must start looking for ways to be yourself in loving people, and you will find that the love of God will draw people to you.

Everyone reading this—if you are filled with the Spirit— has the spirit of evangelism working in you. You must simply become sensitive to the leading of the Spirit so that you may know how you can be used in your unique way to help make disciples in every nation.

Evangelism is not complicated. The heart of discipleship is friendship, friendship with God and friendship with people. If you want to be a soul-winner, you must be a friend-winner first. And we all do that in different ways.

CHAPTER ELEVEN

THE SPIRIT OF EVANGELISM
IN THE CHURCH

I must make one final point before leaving you alone.

As I have said over and over—which is deliberate, by the way—the spirit of evangelism is a spirit that works in all of us as individuals. Yet, when He begins to work effectively in us as individuals, He produces a corporate spirit of evangelism that begins to flow within the church at large. The spirit of evangelism is like beautiful music that is played in perfect harmony when we all find our place in the orchestra.

Now, I need to make clear just what I am saying here. The spirit of evangelism works in us as individuals. We do not want to lose sight of that point after having worked so hard to make it. This means that the Holy Spirit stirs up our unique gifts and abilities and uses them to reach people in a way that only we can. But that cannot be misunderstood to mean that the Holy Spirit works within us in isolation from other believers. Not at all. Individual, yes, Isolated, no. The Spirit that works in us as individuals works through us in concert with others.

None of us have the Spirit alone. By one Spirit we have been baptized into one body (1 Corinthians 12:13). The one Spirit of God plunges us into the one spirit of the church.

There is one body and one Spirit—just as you were called to the one hope that belongs to your call—one Lord, one faith, one baptism, one God and Father of all, who is over all and through all and in all. (Ephesians 4:4-6)

The one body of Christ is formed by one unified Spirit, the Spirit of God in Christ indwelling us as the Holy Spirit. But the Holy Spirit makes us one spirit—the spirit of the church—as our human spirits are joined together.

Paul carefully identifies God as "over all and through all and in all." God is over all: He is *transcendent.* God is through all: He is *mediated.* God is in all: He is *immanent.* Now, we have no problem with God being over us all or in us all, but when we think about God being *through* us all, we lose our bearings a bit and run into the ditch.

Yet it is true. God is *through* us all, which means that He flows throughout the body of Christ as the Holy Spirit joins the regenerated human spirits of believers together in one body, and He flows out of us into the world bringing healing to the nations.

The spirit of the church is made up of the Spirit of God flowing into the spirits of believers, which flow into one another, sometimes easily and sometimes with great difficulty. Sort of like a river—sometimes it flows placidly along, and sometimes it roars in tempestuous rapids. That is the way the spirit of the church flows.

Stop and think about this for a moment. The Spirit of God flows out of Christ as the Holy Spirit into the spirits of those who hear and believe the gospel. The Spirit of God resurrects the spirit of man, and all the latent, dormant human potential that was sown like seed in the soul of man when God first formed him from dust is awakened day by day to blossom in the fullness of human being. The Spirit of God awakens talents and abilities and develops human personality into the multifaceted image of God that finds its unique expression in each individual.

However, that uniqueness is two-dimensional (God and man) until it is brought into spiritual union with others who bear within themselves the complementary aspects of human being that flesh out the image of God in manifold expressions.

What does that mean, you ask? And you should ask just that. Here is what it means. The image of God cannot be fully displayed in one person. Just like a symphony cannot be played by one instrument. It takes an orchestra to play the music to its fullest. Just so, it takes a multitude no man can number to fully manifest the image of God.

This is why Jesus, the singular image of God, is glorified and poured out as the Holy Spirit to dwell within believers. He is the image of God, no doubt, but He is the fully revealed image of God only as He is fully manifest in the church.

The fullness of God can only be seen in the fullness of Christ; the fullness of Christ can only be seen in the fullness of the body of Christ; and the fullness of the body of Christ can only be seen in the fullness of the new creation. Paul describes this as "the fullness of him who fills all in all" (Ephesians 1:23). God is filled up when we are filled up. This is a cycle of fullness that boggles the mind.

So, God fills up Christ who fills up the church, and the church up fills all creation. And this "filling up" includes "filling out." The church "fills out" all the latent potential of God's good creation, a "filling out" that only be fully realized in the resurrection when the "fullness of time" has come. Lord have mercy, this paragraph is chock-full of fullness.

Anyway, the fullness of all things is what salvation is all about. God intends to restore His creation and recover the purpose that Adam lost. This is what God meant when He told Adam to "fill up" the earth. He did not mean for Adam to simply place a warm body in every corner of the world. He meant for Adam to develop all of the resources of earth to the glory of God.

But this is the part that we need to grasp now. This fullness is not only vertical; it is horizontal. This creational fullness not only flows from God to people, but it flows from person to person. When God brings people into spiritual union with one another, they fulfill each other. When two or three agree together, Jesus stands in the midst. The two or three become more together than they could have been alone.

When Jesus fills up the spirit of Bob, and Bob is brought into fellowship with Bill, who is also filled with the Spirit of Jesus, then Bob and Bill are meant to fill up one another. This means that Bob and Bill *must* be one with each other in order to be fully the ones they were meant to be. They must be one with *other-selves* to really become *themselves*.

Now, that may make some of us a tad uncomfortable. We like our space. But in reality, the human race is a mishmash of human spirits, anyway. Get a crowd together, and the spirits of the people in the room will get all mixed up with one another no matter how they try to prevent it, and the result is the spirit of the crowd, the atmosphere of the room. This is why people will do in a crowd what they would never do alone. It is a mob mentality, but it is more than just a mentality. It is the spirit of the crowd. Many individual spirits flow together to form one unified spirit.

Back to the symphony metaphor. The violin cannot play the music alone. The violin needs the cello, and the cello needs the violin. And they both need the timpani and the trumpets. The violin becomes more violin-ish when it is played in harmony with the rest of the orchestra. The violin is filled up and filled out by the other instruments.

Now, you have guessed by now that this is a favorite subject of mine and that I really could go on like this for years. Really, I could. But I must drag this aspiring magnum opus back to the original point. The spirit of evangelism that works in you as an individual must work in concert with the spirit of evangelism in others until the spirit of evangelism in us becomes the spirit of evangelism in the church.

You must reach people as only you can reach people. But when you start reaching people the way that only you can reach people and I start reaching people the way that only I can reach people—which is the only way that I *can* reach people—then your way of reaching people will complement my way of reaching people, and our way of reaching people will become the way that our church reaches people. Get that?

So. Here is the bottom line. If you or I fail to reach people the way that only we can reach people, then our church will never reach people in the full spectrum of all the ways that it should reach people.

This means that if I do not permit the spirit of evangelism to flow in me in concert with you, then the spirit of evangelism in our church will always be lacking in fullness. If

61

I do not play my violin the way that only I can play my violin, and if I do not play my violin in harmony with the way that only you can play your cello, then the parts that my violin and your cello should play will always be missing from the music.

What we are looking for here is the spirit of evangelism that works in each of us to become the spirit of evangelism that takes over the church until the church *in toto* is swept up in the purpose of reaching the lost.

CONCLUSION

Let's see if we can steer this dinghy to pier. Been a much longer voyage than we set out to sail, but, hopefully, the trip has been worth the effort.

The spirit of evangelism is the Spirit of God that works within our human spirit to develop our individual witness in concert with the spirit of fellow believers that flow together into the one spirit of the local church until it is full of the spirit of evangelism.

You have the spirit of evangelism in you. It is the Spirit of Christ, the ultimate Evangelist. You simply must learn to allow the Spirit of evangelism to develop in your spirit so that your style of evangelism is Jesus-style evangelism individualized in you.

Then, you must allow your spirit to be harmonized with the spirits of fellow believers until your spirit of evangelism is heightened and strengthened by their spirit of evangelism.

When this occurs, the church you attend will begin to see marked increase in the spirit of evangelism that characterizes the congregation. In this way, your local church will mature in its own approach to reaching people in your community. All because the Spirit of evangelism is unleashed in you, in your fellow believers and in your church.

The spirit of evangelism reaches people through "Evangelism Jesus-style." Which means, if you got hold of what we talked about earlier, evangelism done a thousand different ways. We only discussed about eight different ways that Jesus did evangelism, but as we all grow in our own unique way of reaching people, evangelism Jesus-style takes on an infinite range of possible approaches to discipling people. Evangelism Jesus-style is evangelism done your style harmonized with your brother's style until evangelism becomes the church's style.

Jesus said, "By this my Father is glorified, that you bear much fruit and so prove to be my disciples." (John 15:8) We prove we are disciples by making disciples. Just as Jesus was declared to be the Son of God with power by the resurrection from the dead, so we are declared to be the sons of God by the witness of Christ's resurrection that lives in us.

As we become witnesses of Christ's resurrection, our testimony also becomes the proof that we are His disciples. It works both ways. Our witness proves that God is true, and our witness proves that we are His disciples. So, it is no light thing to dismiss our responsibility to make disciples.

Everyone must be evangelistic in order to confirm that we are His disciples. But just before the guilt sets in again, let me remind you: I am speaking of becoming the witness that God called *you* to be, not the witness that God called your brother to be. All we are asked to do is to allow the Spirit of evangelism, the living Witness within us, to testify of Christ's life by living His life in our unique way. Simply be who God called you to be, and seek opportunities to be you in a way that draws men and women to Christ.

Jesus also said,

> You did not choose me, but I chose you and appointed you that you should go and bear fruit and that your fruit should abide, so that whatever you ask the Father in my name, he may give it to you. (John 15:16)

You are called to bear fruit. Indeed, you *must* bear fruit. But do not expect that you will bear apples if you are an orange tree. Ask the Father in the name of Jesus to let you bear the fruit that He has gifted you to bear. Then, let the Spirit of evangelism work in you until it is flowing like a river through the church.